T0023650

THE MEDICARE TIMELINE

YOUR STEP-BY-STEP GUIDE TO TURNING 65

written by
THOMAS BRZEZINSKI &
CRAIG HANSEN

The goal of this book is to present a concise understanding of what you need to know when it comes to Medicare, to help simplify the process, and to highlight the common mistakes to avoid. Reliable information and advice when making such an important decision are what Medicare beneficiaries need most, and in the following pages we will uncover the untold secrets that will help you best navigate this complex decision.

The Medicare Timeline

Your Step-by-Step Guide to Turning 65

ISBN: 979-8-35092-968-3

Contents

CHAPTER 1.

Introduction:
The Initial Enrollment Period

If you're turning 65, Medicare requires important steps to be taken, some of which you may find confusing, such as:

- How do I enroll?

- When do I enroll?

- What are my coverage choices?

Not taking the correct steps at the right time, or misunderstanding the above, can cost you with:

- Penalties

- Coverage Delays

- Losing Guaranteed Issue Rights

Understanding The Initial Enrollment Period:

When it comes to enrolling in Medicare, like most things in life, **timing is everything**.

As you approach your 65th birthday, you will have 7 months to sign up for Medicare. That includes, but isn't limited to Part A, Part

B, Medigap (aka supplement, stand-alone prescription plans), and medicare advantage plans.

During this **Initial Enrollment Period (IEP)** it is important to understand that action must be taken by you no matter your situation. You have to choose among the following three options:

1. Enroll in Medicare Part A and B (this will happen automatically if you are collecting Social Security Benefits).

2. Enroll in Part A only.

3. Waive both Part A and Part B. Your specific situation will determine 1, 2, or 3.

To be clear, your IEP period consists of three months before you turn 65, your birthday month, plus three months after – a total of 7 months to make your choice. For example, if you turn 65 on February 12, your IEP runs from November 1 through May 31.

Curveball: If your birthday is on the 1st of the month, everything is shifted one month earlier. For example, if your birthday is April 1st, your IEP will begin in December and your Medicare start date will be March 1st.

There are three ways you can sign up for Medicare Part A and Part B:

1. Visit your local Social Security Office in person.

2. Call the main Social Security phone number 1-800-772-1213.

3. Visit the SSA website WWW.SSA.GOV. and enroll online.

Jersey Insurance Solutions strongly recommends taking action quickly to allow the time needed for enrollments to be processed. Do not be fooled by the seemingly long 7-month time period, you should focus on your decision within the first 2 months of your IEP.

Keep in mind: Jersey Insurance Solutions is here to help guide you through this process. However, ultimately, enrollment in Part A and Part B of Medicare is YOUR responsibility.

Scan this QR code to download our free exclusive step-by-step enrollment guide to help you enroll online.

Working Past Age 65?

Folks working past 65 are more common than ever these days. The biggest question we get from those not ready or able to hang up the towel is, "Do I still need to enroll in Medicare Part A and Part B? The short answer: it depends. Here's a breakdown:

Sign up for Medicare Part A and Part B if:

- If the employer from which you or your spouse receive your group health insurance has UNDER 20 employees. If so, Medicare is your Primary insurance, and your employer's Group Health Plan is your Secondary. In this case, you must sign up for Part A and Part B. Not signing up for Medicare Part A and Part B would result in denied claims by your Group Health Insurance.

Sign up for Medicare Part A only if:

- If the employer where you or your spouse receive group health insurance from has OVER 20 employees. In this scenario, you can potentially delay Part B since your Group Health Plan would be Primary and Medicare Secondary.

Waive Part A and Part B if:

- If your employer has OVER 20 employees and you are actively contributing to an HSA (Health Savings Account). Actively contributing to an HSA while on any Part of Medicare is a no-no.

Medicare Pro Tip #3: Be careful if you decide to call Social Security and ask for their advice on this. However well-intentioned, Social Security will advise if you are actively working and covered by your employer's group health insurance plan that you do not need to enroll in Medicare and you can delay your Medicare enrollment. That's not entirely accurate and can lead to coverage delays and penalties. We advise you to confirm with your employer or HR that your current Group Health Plan meets credibility requirements. If your current plan does not meet credibility requirements, you could face late enrollment penalties in the future if you delay Medicare.

CHAPTER 2.

The Special Enrollment Period:

Up to this point, everything we have discussed pertains to your 1st step. Your Medicare Part A and B enrollment, rules, and procedures. As we move along, we will review your secondary coverage options – Medicare Supplement (Medigap), prescription plans, as well as medicare advantage plans.

Now that you have a clear picture of what you need to do as you enter your IEP, what happens when you are beyond age 65 and you retire or lose your employer Group Health Plan coverage?

What Is The Special Enrollment Period:

When this happens, you will have a Special Enrollment Period (SEP). The SEP allows you to sign up for Medicare outside the initial enrollment period without penalty. Let's focus on those working past age 65 and signing up for Medicare using special enrollment periods.

Assuming you signed up for Part A only during your IEP, SEPs offer an 8-month window to enroll in Medicare Part B. Your 8-month SEP begins the date you retire or lose employer coverage as an active employee, whichever happens 1st.

The SEP will also allow you to enroll in secondary options like Medigap, part D, or Part C without penalties. But SEPs can be tricky. While you have an 8-month window to enroll in Part B, you only have a 6-month window to enroll in a Medigap (aka supplement) without having to answer health questions, and 63 days to enroll in Part D (stand-alone RX plan), or Part C (medicare advantage plan). You may face late enrollment penalties when going beyond the above enrollment windows.

We can hear some saying: "What do you mean without having to answer health questions?"

Yes, it's true. During SEP periods you can enroll in a supplement plan without having to answer medical questions and receive coverage automatically at the best standard rate possible. However, if you decline a Medicare Supplement during either your IEP or SEP and decide to apply in the future, your acceptance is not guaranteed and you will need to answer medical questions. The application will be reviewed through an underwriting process and the insurance company can deny you coverage.

> *Medicare Pro Tip #4: COBRA does not allow you to delay your Medicare enrollment. Remember, your 8-month enrollment window starts when you retire or lose your group health insurance coverage. Whichever comes first.*

A Brief History Of Medicare Part A and Part B:

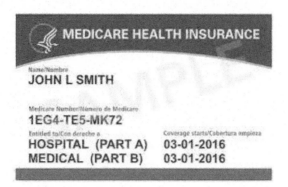

Medicare Part A and Part B, also known as Original Medicare, are the foundation of Medicare as we know it.

Part A = In-patient hospital stays, skilled nursing, home health/hospice care. It includes:

- A hospital admission deductible per benefit period.

- Daily co-pays for skilled nursing and hospital confinement may apply for extended stays.

- Premium-free as long as you or your spouse have worked 40 quarters or more.

Part B = Doctors, Testing, Outpatient Services:

- Has an annual deductible.

- Part B covers 80% of the Medicare-approved services after the annual deductible. The 20% you pay has NO CAP or MAXIMUM.

- Part B does have a monthly premium, an amount that is determined by your income. The higher your income, the higher the cost.

Scan the QR code to review the Income Related Monthly Adjustment Amounts (IRMMA) to determine your Part B premium.

What does Part A and Part B NOT cover?

- Part A: Deductible and daily hospital co-pays

- Part B: 20% Co-insurance, annual deductible

The bottom line: Medicare Part A and B have many coverage gaps. Just having those is simply not enough coverage in today's healthcare world. The solution is secondary coverage that covers those gaps in Parts A and B.

> *Medicare Pro Tip #5: Enrolling in Medicare Part A and B can be confusing. We recommend consulting a local professional to help discover the best way to enroll and when. Like we always say timing with Medicare is everything.*

Your Medicare Options:

There are basically **2 options** available after signing up for Medicare Part A and Part B:

- Option 1 = Medicare Supplement (aka Medigap) and Part D prescription plan.
- Option 2 = Medicare Advantage Plan (aka Part C).

Option 1 - Medicare Supplements

Medicare Supplements, also known as Medigap plans, fill in the coverage gaps left by Medicare Part A and Part B. These supplements step in to cover what your primary Medicare doesn't.

> *FYI...one of the great components of a Medicare supplement is that there are NO NETWORKS to think about. That means you have coverage anywhere that accepts Medicare across the country. With a supplement, you no longer need to worry if a doctor is in-network or not.*

CHAPTER 3.

Supplement Plan G Versus Plan N

The first important thing to know is all Medicare Supplement plans are standardized.

This means that if you choose to enroll in Plan G, the coverage will be identical regardless of the insurance company you select. The same goes for Plan N. The only potential differences are the insurance company name, cost, and any annual rate increases.

So what is Plan G? Right now Plan G is the top-end supplement you can enroll in if you turn 65 after 1/1/2020. It provides ultimate coverage for beneficiaries covering almost everything original medicare Part A and B does not cover. The only out-of-pocket expense you would have is the 1-time annual Part B deductible, (for example, the 2023 Part B annual deductible is $226, but is subject to change year to year). After paying this annual Part B deductible, you pay nothing. Plan G also picks up the remaining out-of-pocket costs, which include doctor co-pays.

Conversely, Plan N is your next best option after G. This plan gives all the major benefits of enrolling in a supplement, reducing the monthly premium for the enrollee. If you are budget-conscious but still want to have the freedom to see any provider, this is a great option.

Like with Plan G, and Plan N you will need to pay the Part B deductible, but also would be responsible for a $20 co-pay to visit the doctor and a $50 copay for emergency room visits where you are not admitted to the hospital.

It's crucial to be aware that Plan N does not provide coverage for Part B excess charges. While these charges are relatively rare, it's essential to exercise caution when seeking care from providers who accept Medicare, but may not accept the payment rates set by Medicare.

Medicare supplement key takeaways:

1. No networks. You have the freedom to see any provider that accepts Medicare.

2. Must pay monthly premiums.

3. Least amount of out-of-pocket costs and or financial exposure.

To learn more about Plan G vs. Plan N. scan the QR code below to download our free guide.

CHAPTER 4.

Part D Stand-Alone Prescription Plans

It is important to remember that when enrolling in Medicare Part A and B, it does not include prescription drug coverage, and the enrollment is not automatic. This means even after enrolling in Medicare Part A and B with a supplement, you still need to find an additional plan option to help cover drugs.

Part D is not mandatory, but if you do not enroll you can receive a late enrollment penalty that can be for your lifetime. It can be upwards of a 12% penalty per year for every year you were not enrolled. This penalty is in addition to your monthly Part D plan premium. Trust us, you don't want to make this mistake.

We recommend enrolling in a Prescription Part D plan even if you do not currently take any medications.

In addition, Part D is only offered through private insurance companies and you must have Part A and or B to qualify and the coverage varies from plan to plan. Not only do the plans vary from one to another but they can change every year. Each plan has a list of drugs that it covers and that list can change from year to year.

Cost sharing for Part D plans simplified:

1. **Annual Deductible:** Many plans have a yearly deductible. You pay this amount before the plan starts helping with drug costs. May only be for specific drugs that are not deductible exempt.

2. **Initial Coverage:** After the deductible, you enter the initial coverage phase. Here, you and your plan share the drug costs. You pay a copayment or coinsurance, and the plan covers the rest.

3. **Coverage Gap** (Donut Hole): If your drug costs reach a certain limit, you enter the coverage gap (often called 'the donut hole'). During this phase, you pay a higher percentage (25%) of the drug costs until you reach a set limit.

4. **Catastrophic Coverage:** Once you spend a certain amount out of pocket, you move to the catastrophic coverage stage. Here, your costs drop significantly for both generic and brand-name drugs.

In simple terms, you start with a deductible and then share costs in the initial coverage phase. If drug expenses go high, you temporarily pay more in the coverage gap, but it gets better in the catastrophic phase.

CHAPTER 5.

Understanding Medicare Advantage Part C

Understanding Medicare Advantage (Part C) can be confusing. Medicare Advantage plans are private health insurance plans that are approved by Medicare. Medicare Advantage Plans combine Part A, Part B, and most often Part D into one plan with a network of providers.

Medicare Advantage Plans operate in a way similar to group health insurance plans. When you have a Medicare Advantage plan, you use it to get medical treatment, and you'll have costs like copays or deductibles.

However, there's a catch – Medicare Advantage plans often come with limitations. They may restrict you to specific service areas and require you to use a network of doctors and hospitals, which can be different from the flexibility of Original Medicare.

Remember, these are private plans approved by Medicare.

Another thing to keep in mind is that these plans can change from year to year, including the doctors and hospitals they cover.

But here's the silver lining: many Medicare Advantage plans don't have a monthly premium, making them an attractive option for those looking to save on premium costs. While you'll still need to pay the

Part B premium, your Medicare Advantage plan takes center stage as your primary and secondary insurance.

Pros of Medicare Advantage (Part C) Plans:

1. **All-in-One Coverage**: Medicare Advantage plans often include all Medicare Part A, Part B, and Part D prescription drug coverage in one plan, simplifying your healthcare.

2. **Additional Benefits:** Many plans offer extra benefits like dental, vision, hearing, and wellness programs that Original Medicare doesn't cover.

3. **Potentially Lower Costs**: Premiums for Medicare Advantage plans can be low, and some plans have $0 premiums.

4. **Out-of-Pocket Maximum**: Medicare Advantage plans have annual out-of-pocket maximums, limiting your potential healthcare expenses.

Cons of Medicare Advantage (Part C) Plans:

1. **Network Limitations**: You are required to use a specific network of doctors and hospitals, limiting your choice of healthcare providers.

2. **Changing Plans Annually**: Plan benefits, costs, and in-network providers can change from year to year, potentially affecting your coverage.

3. **Prior Authorization**: Some procedures and medications may require prior authorization from the plan, leading to delays in care.

4. **Geographic Restrictions**: Coverage may be limited to a specific service area, which can be an issue if you travel frequently or have multiple residences.

5. **Limited Flexibility**: Unlike Original Medicare, which allows you to see any Medicare-approved provider, Medicare Advantage plans often have stricter rules about where you can receive care.

To learn more about Option 1 (Medicare Supplement and Part D) Vs. Option 2 (Medicare Advantage - Part C) scan the QR below to download our comparison breakdown.

CHAPTER 6.

Additional Election Periods To Understand

The AEP, or Annual Enrollment Period, runs from October 15th to December 7th each year. During this time, you have the opportunity to review and make changes to your Medicare Advantage or Part D prescription drug plans. These changes become effective on January 1st of the following year.

Think of it as the time when you can give your Medicare Advantage plan or Part D prescription drug coverage a check-up. If you want to switch plans, add or drop prescription drug coverage, or make any adjustments to your healthcare choices, the Annual Enrollment Period is your chance to do it. Your new plan choices will kick in on the first day of the upcoming year.

You can change the following during this time:

- Switch from one Part D prescription drug plan or Medicare Advantage to another.
- Switch from original Medicare to Medicare Advantage or vice versa.

After the Annual Enrollment Period (AEP) closes out on Dec 7th, you will have another opportunity to adjust your plan again. The Open Enrollment Period (OEP) begins January 1 through March 31 for people to make additional elections or change the following. Think of the OEP as a time to change your Medicare Advantage Plan if you missed the AEP or you changed your plan during the AEP and are unhappy with the selection you made and would like to change it again.

- Medicare Advantage to Medicare Advantage
- Medicare Advantage back to original Medicare

CHAPTER 7.

Timing With Medicare Is Everything...Avoid These Common Pitfalls Of Medicare

As we said, when it comes to Medicare *timing is everything* and it is essential to understand the timeframe in which you need to make these important decisions.

To avoid making the mistakes and falling trap to the pitfalls of Medicare we recommend using a trusted local resource like Jersey Insurance Solutions that can help keep you on track. Remember everyone's personal Medicare situation is different and it is important to seek out and find out the best solutions for you.

So what are common Medicare pitfalls?

Pitfall #1: Missing Important Enrollment Deadlines

When you turn 65, your initial enrollment period is crucial to grasp. During this time, you need to take action to ensure you're covered. This period spans seven months in total: the three months before your 65th birthday month, your birthday month itself, and the three months following your 65th birthday.

Our recommendation is not to wait until your 65th birthday month to make decisions. Using the three months before your birthday allows you to make elections and choices without causing delays in your coverage. Missing this window can lead to lifetime penalties and coverage gaps.

Here are some key points to remember:

- If you're already receiving Social Security benefits before turning 65, you'll be automatically enrolled in Medicare Part A and Part B. However, this doesn't include secondary coverage (supplement) or a Part D prescription drug plan.

- If you plan to keep working past age 65 and stay on your employer's group health insurance, you might still need to enroll in Medicare.

- Even if you choose to waive Part A and Part B for specific reasons, we strongly advise understanding the rationale behind your decision and having a plan in place for when you decide to enroll in the Parts you are currently postponing.

Medicare Pro Tip #6: Avoid Cobra When Retiring: A crucial tip: if you're over age 65 and decide to retire and your employer offers you COBRA coverage, think twice. We've seen cases where people lost their special enrollment period and guaranteed issue rights because they opted for COBRA over the eight-month window. This decision prevented them from enrolling in Medicare Part A and/or Part B on time.

Late enrollments are something you want to steer clear of. Missing deadlines can result in losing coverage until the next general or annual election period.

Additionally, lifetime penalties could apply based on the duration you were without coverage. If you apply for a Medicare Supplement after missing the Part B enrollment period, you'll likely have to answer medical questions and undergo underwriting for acceptance into the plan. Your coverage in the supplement won't be guaranteed.

Late enrollment in Part D also comes with a lifetime penalty. The penalty amount is determined by the number of months you were without Part D coverage from the time you were supposed to enroll. This penalty persists indefinitely and increases the longer you go without Part D.

Remember, understanding Medicare enrollment time-frames is crucial to avoiding penalties and coverage gaps. Missing these deadlines can have long-term consequences, so it's essential to take action during your initial enrollment period.

Pitfall #2 - Losing Guaranteed Issue Rights To Medicare Supplement Plans

Medicare supplements, also known as Medigap plans, play a vital role by covering the costs that Medicare Part A and Part B don't. They help with deductibles, copayments, and coinsurance, offering you peace of mind.

Here's the catch: getting accepted for a Medicare Supplement is not guaranteed unless you apply during specific open enrollment periods, which we outlined above. If you delay or miss these open enrollment windows, you'll likely have to go through a process called medical underwriting.

Medical underwriting involves answering health-related questions, and the insurance company may charge you higher rates or even deny you coverage altogether based on your health status.

To secure your Medicare Supplement plan at the best possible rate and without the uncertainty of underwriting, it's essential to take action during your open enrollment periods. This step is especially crucial if you have chronic health conditions, as it ensures you get the plan you want at the most favorable rate available.

Pitfall #3: Failing To Review Your Medicare Drug Plan Or Medicare Advantage Plan Annually

Another crucial aspect of managing your Medicare effectively is staying on top of your plan's changes. Here's why:

One of the valuable services that a trusted insurance agent provides is helping clients with annual plan reviews and adjustments. Skipping this step can be costly. It's easy to assume that since your plan covered everything well in the past, it will remain the same in the future. However, that's not always the case.

Part D drug plans and Medicare Advantage benefits can change from year to year, as can the list of covered medications. That's why it's crucial to review your plan during the annual election period, either with your agent or independently.

If you don't have a dedicated agent, we recommend finding a local resource you trust to assist you in making the best decision for your medical needs. Any changes you don't make during this period will have to wait until the following year.

Missing your annual review and potentially failing to adjust your drug plan can be a significant oversight. To avoid this mistake, mark your calendar and schedule a plan review with a trusted local resource or your insurance agent to ensure your coverage aligns with your current healthcare needs.

CHAPTER 8.

Your Confident Medicare Journey

Congratulations! You've navigated the labyrinth of Medicare intricacies, pitfalls, and choices outlined in this book. By reaching this point, you've empowered yourself with knowledge that will undoubtedly serve you well in your Medicare journey.

Remember, knowledge is the key to confidence, and you're now armed with insights that many Medicare beneficiaries lack. You've learned about the critical Initial Enrollment Period (IEP) and Special Enrollment Periods (SEPs), understanding their nuances, and making informed decisions within those timeframes. This understanding is paramount in avoiding penalties, coverage gaps, and delays that could otherwise arise from missing enrollment windows.

Furthermore, you've become familiar with the different paths available after enrolling in Medicare Part A and Part B. Whether you're exploring Medicare Supplements (Medigap) to cover the gaps, diving into stand-alone prescription plans (Part D), or considering the intricacies of Medicare Advantage (Part C), you're equipped to make choices that align with your unique needs and preferences.

In this book, you've grasped the significance of reviewing your Medicare plan annually. A vigilant review ensures that your chosen plan continues to meet your evolving healthcare needs, safeguarding you against unexpected coverage changes or costs.

Remember, You Are Not In This Alone:

At this point, you might be wondering about your next steps. We want to assure you that you don't have to navigate this path alone. Jersey Insurance Solutions stands ready as your trusted partner. Our experienced team is dedicated to providing personalized guidance, answering your questions, and helping you make the most informed decisions for your Medicare coverage.

The journey to mastering Medicare doesn't end here, it's ongoing. As your needs evolve, new questions might arise. But armed with the knowledge you've acquired, you're well-prepared to tackle these challenges.

Medicare doesn't have to be a daunting puzzle. It's a valuable resource that ensures you receive the healthcare you deserve throughout your golden years.

We believe that every Medicare beneficiary deserves peace of mind, confidence, and the freedom to make the best healthcare decisions. With the insights from this book and the assistance of Jersey Insurance Solutions, you're on your way to enjoying a simple, seamless, and confident Medicare experience. Welcome to a brighter, informed future with Medicare!

About The Authors

Tom and Craig have been in the health insurance industry for over a decade, helping individuals and businesses find the best solution for their own health insurance needs. Their mantra since entering the often challenging insurance business remains to be "put the clients' needs above all else and give them the best possible experience."

Their journey as business partners began in 2010 when both were working exclusively, but independently, representing Aflac, the leading producer of supplemental health insurance benefits. The two quickly found their perspective on the industry and goals for the future were aligned, and the rest is history.

Working as a team, they've helped thousands of people protect themselves with innovative products that protect against the rising costs of cancer, disability, accidents, and hospitalization. But they also knew there was more to be done, which led to a deep immersion in the health insurance benefits needs of small businesses and their employees. They quickly learned many small businesses struggle to find comprehensive employer-based group health plans at an affordable price for their employees. Providing group health insurance solutions for small to mid-size businesses became the next chapter in their insurance career.

As Tom and Craig's expertise in the space grew, so did requests to help customers navigate the complex and confusing world of Medicare, which requires experience to successfully help folks entering into the system understand and navigate the process.

*After the pandemic, Tom and Craig rebranded the company **Jersey Insurance Solutions** and seized the opportunity to make a real difference in people's lives by guiding them to the best Medicare options for their needs.*

*If you enjoyed the book but would like to have more clarification please join our free Medicare 101 Webinar to join or watch on demand please scan the QR code above to register

Want to learn further from Tom and Craig through a one-on-one review? Scan the below code to schedule an appointment with the authors and let us help you create your own personal Medicare timeline.